Scratching the Surface

Justine Cope

Scratching the Surface
A play in one act

First Published in Great Britain in 2018 by Beercott Books.

Copyright: © Justine Cope 2018

ISBN: 978-1-9997429-6-6

Justine Cope has asserted her rights to be identified as the author of this book.

Title is fully protected under copyright. All rights, including professional and amateur stage production, recitation, lecturing, public reading, motion picture, radio broadcasting, television and the rights of translation into foreign languages are strictly reserved.

A catalogue record of this book is available from the British Library.

No one shall make any changes to the play for the purpose of production. No part of this book may be reproduced, stored in a retrieval system, or transmitted in any form, by any means, now known or yet to be invented. This includes mechanical, electronic, photocopying, recording, videotaping, or otherwise, without the prior written permission of the publisher. No one shall upload this title, or part of this title, to social media websites.

Professional and amateur producers are hereby warned that title is subject to a licencing fee. Publication of this play does not imply availability for performance. Both amateurs and professionals considering a production are strongly advised to apply to the agent before starting rehearsals, advertising, or booking a theatre. A licence fee must be paid whether the title is presented for charity or gain and whether or not admission is charged.

Worldwide licence enquiries for this title should be directed to:
licensing@beercottbooks.co.uk.
Title subject to availability.

---

www.beercottbooks.co.uk

Beercott

AUTHOR'S NOTE

Scratching the Surface offers flexible casting for Youth Groups. Characters can be Male / Female or any combination of the two, it also offers opportunity for doubling/ combining roles for smaller casts, ensuring the characters of The Wise, Rock, Jam, Meil, Cub and Wiz remain consistent. The play allows for additions of music to aid smooth and interesting transitions and physical theatre to enact the quatrains. Staging should be adaptable and interchangeable to allow swift movement between different areas of the bunker. Costuming can be as simplistic or elaborate as the production team choose. The original production incorporated a steam-punk theme, with individualised elements for each character to reflect their identity.

ABOUT NOSTRADAMUS

Michel de Nostredame, usually referred to as 'Nostradamus', was a French physician and apothecary. His book *'Les Propheties'* published in 1955, is a collection of 942 poetic 'quatrains' which allegedly predict future events. He is widely regarded as the most influential 'seer' of the renaissance period and his quatrains are regularly attributed to world events from the invasion of Hitler in World War 2 to the atomic bombings in Hiroshima.

ABOUT THE AUTHOR

Justine Cope is a Creative Arts and Drama Practitioner, Director and Lecturer in Education. Her passion for writing stems from her love of creativity and devising, scripting and directing drama, theatre and arts projects.

She works with numerous educational settings and arts organisations to design and deliver creative provision, in addition to being a Creative Director of Fusion Performance Arts, in Staffordshire.

Justine has written several award winning One Act Plays for Youth/Young Performers which have been performed as part of The All England Theatre Festival including 'The Trial of Rattenfanger' and 'From Ashes to Coals'.

ORIGINAL PRODUCTION

The play was first performed by 'Fusion Actors Lab' as part of the Tamworth Hastilow One Act Play Festival on 22nd March 2017 and subsequently performed on 25th March at The Mitchell Arts Centre, Stoke on Trent as part of the Stoke on Trent One Act Play Festival.

The original cast was as follows:

The Wise

MIN: Jasmine Newbold

FOX: Isabelle Foxall

The Chosen

ROCK: Holly Stones

KEL: Kelsie Bond

AL: Alisha Murray

MEIL: Amelia Wray

JAM: Rebekah Howard

CUB: James Howard

ILY: Lily Brassington

LUCE: Lucy Harbour

WIZ: Willow Gregory

ZEE: Zoe Hunter

HAM: Evie Hammer-Bailey

LIS: Lois Heath

DEE: Jodie Birks

LION: Leo Skelton

POP: Poppy Pickering

BEC: Rebecca Wooliscroft

CHARACTERS

The Wise (played by older children or adults):

Min

Fox

The Chosen (children 8-15yrs):

ROCK: generally accepted as the 'Leader' of the Chosen

KEL

AL

MEIL: Cocky and confrontational

JAM: Smart and witty

CUB: The youngest of the group

ILY

LUCE

WIZ: Serious and knowledgeable

ZEE: Excitable and enthusiastic

HAM

LIS

DEE

LION

POP

BEC

SCRATCHING THE SURFACE.

The Wise and Chosen stand looking up

VOICE: For seven days the great star will burn,
          The cloud shall make two suns to appear:
          The big mastiff will howl all night
          When the great pontiff changes country.

The company respond to the quatrain as if a form of worship and disperse in military fashion. The space is transformed into a recreation area.

The Chosen are sitting pondering their existence.

HAM: We're nothing more than moles living under ground.

DEE: We are nothing like moles – moles are small black creatures!

POP: Yeah, they have four legs – we only have two, and they can see in the dark!

KEL: So they say…

LIS: Who says?

KEL: The Wise – think about have we ever seen a mole?

HAM: Well no, not actually seen one, but I've seen pictures!

KEL: So, how do you actually know that they exist?

POP: We did it in lessons, didn't we?

MEIL: (*mimicking*) We did it in lessons, didn't we (*laughs*).

KEL: We've only got their word for it?

LIS: What do you mean?

MEIL: Do you believe everything they say?

ROCK: Shut up you two, stop stirring things!

LIS: Yes, of course I do.

JAM: Course she does, she's a bit (*indicates that LIS is loopy*) you know!

BEC: Don't be so mean Jam.

MEIL: Do you ever wonder how we got here?

LIS: The Wise brought us.

KEL: The Wise brought us… the wise brought us – course they did!

ILY: Does that mean the Wise are our parents?

LUCE: I don't think so, otherwise we would call them Mum or Dad?

AL: Perhaps we are orphans?

CUB: What's an Orphan?

WIZ: (*offering a definition*) Orphan – A child who has been abandoned or whose parents are both dead.

KEL: Dead, deceased, gone!

MEIL: Nice!

AL: So, what are we orphaned or abandoned? (*pause, she turns to ROCK*) Rock?

Rock ignores her

AL: Rock, what are we?

ROCK: What's it matter, we're just here aren't we?

MEIL: Yes, but aren't you curious Rock? (*ROCK ignores her*)

BEC: What's the point in being curious, it isn't going to get us anywhere is it – eh Rock?

AL: I think we're orphans.

MEIL: What all of us? Definitely abandoned I'd say.

WIZ: Abandoned, discarded, thrown away…

JAM: Der…de….derrr!!!

HAM: That's a terrible thing to say.

POP: Rock, what do you think.

ROCK: I think you'd better all shut up!

LUCE: Who's rattled her cage?

AL: She's been moody all day.

POP: She's always moody.

ROCK: I'm not moody, I just can't see the point of talking about it, we're here aren't we? Been here as long as we can remember- haven't we?

KEL: Doesn't mean it's always been that way.

DEE: Doesn't it?

ROCK: Can any of you lot remember being anywhere else... (*she waits for a response, but none is forthcoming*) so there you go, this is it - we're here, and I don't think that is going to change - so there!

POP: It's fate I say, that's why we're here.

LUCE: The Wise say we shouldn't question our existence, we should accept the path that has been chosen for us.

JAM: Now where's the fun in that?

MEIL: We have a right to know where we came from, don't we?

AL: She who questions, may receive answers she does not wish to seek.

DEE: That's what the Wise say.

KEL: I just want to know more that's all.

ROCK: We all want to know more Kel, but there is a right way of going about it! Do you want the Wise to be suspicious?

MEIL: Oooo she speaks; you are curious then Rock? Thought for a minute you'd gone soft on us.

ROCK: Not soft Meil, I just like to plan things and not go wading in like you.

Zee enters excitedly

ZEE: Guys, you'll never guess what I just heard?

DEE: What?

LUCE: Lessons are cancelled?

LIS: There's a mole in the bunker?

HAM: Christmas is coming?

JAM: The end of the world is nigh?

Bec: (*Sarcastically*) Bit late for that isn't it?

POP: They're at it again

ILLY: Are you going to tell us or what?

General other banter pursues

ZEE: I would if I could get a work in edgeways!

LION: Well….?

ZEE: It's the Wise they scratched the surface again last night.

MEIL: What did they find?

ZEE: Dunno - but better than that, I heard them talking about the portal code.

LEO: and…….?

ZEE: And I wrote it down, I have the portal code! So, who fancies a little journey to the surface with me?

JAM: I'm well up for it!

General excitement as others indicate their wish to explore

ROCK: Hang on, settle down – do you want the Wise to hear us?

KEL: No, Rock

ROCK: We have to plan this carefully, be prepared - so as not to alert suspicion.

POP: So, what are we going to do?

Act 1 SCRATCHING THE SURFACE

ROCK: Al, you remember the communicators we looked at in lessons?

AL: Yes, Rock?

ROCK: You and Lion need to get hold of them, they will be vital if we want to scratch the surface. Now I suggest a few of us at first and the others keep look out.

BEC: I deffo think I should go!

JAM: Why should you go? The jobs obviously mine! I'm buff, brave and too cool for school!

BEC: Yeah right, dream on, more like short, stupid and bit wet behind the ears! You're so full of yourself Jam!

JAM: Whatever!

AL: I'm the eldest, so I think its best if I go first.

MEIL: (*confidently*) Yeah, well I know things.....

LUCE: Like what Meil?

MEIL: Things, just things.

POP: That's not fair

HAM: I want to go….

LIS: Me too!

ROCK: Well, we can't all go at once, they'll get suspicious.

MEIL: I think it's safer all together.

ILY: Yeah, we can look out for each other.

General agreement

ROCK: Ok have it your way, but if anyone lets it slip then….

KEL: (*interrupting*) We get the picture, so what's the plan Rock?

ROCK: Al and Lion will take the communicators from the classroom, it's lights out at ten tonight so we'll meet in the airlock at 10.15. Everyone arrange your beds to look like you are sleeping and be as quiet as possible. Remember, we must not arouse suspicion.

AL: Yes, Rock.

POP: It's almost 9am Rock.

ROCK: Right, off to lessons now and don't breathe a word.

The space is transformed into an 'Assembly Room'

The Chosen enter in military fashion and take out their digital learning devices. The ensuing 'lesson' is formal and fast paced. The Wise can either take it in turns to ask questions or speak in unison.

WISE: Prediction?

MEIL: Prediction: A forecast, prognosis or prophecy.

WISE: Prophecy?

BEC: Prophecy – A prediction of what will happen in the future.

WISE: Future?

POP: Future – The period of time following what is now!

WISE: Time?

ROCK: Time -The indefinite continued progress of existence and events in the past, present, and future - regarded as a whole.

WISE: History?

HAM: History - The Study of past events

WISE: (*pushing for a deeper definition*) History?

DEE: History - A continuous, typically chronological, record of important or public events or of a particular trend or institution

WISE: Philosopher?

AL: A person engaged in philosophy.

MIN: Detail?

ZEE: Philosopher - A thinker, theorist, hypothesiser, guru.

FOX: Example?

Act 1 SCRATCHING THE SURFACE 17

CHOSEN: Michele de Nostradame. (*groans*)

MIN: Better known as?

Chosen: Nostradamus!

MEIL: Not the quatrains again.

FOX: Excuse me?

MEIL: It's always the quatrains!

CUB: Quatrains?

WIZ: (*proudly offering a definition*) Quatrain – stanza or poem consisting of four lines.

CUB: What?

LION: Nostradamus used the quatrains to make predictions about the future.

MIN: Well done Lion, glad to see that you have being paying attention, so what is your favorite quatrain?

LION: The young lion, shall overcome the older,
On the field of battle, by singular duel;
Through armour of gold, his eye will be pierced,
two wounds in one, then to die a cruel death.

FOX: Definition anyone?

WIZ: Nostradamus is explaining that the young Lion is….

FOX: (*interrupting*) Anyone other than Wiz care to give it a try?

DEE: He is talking about the royal duel in 1559. The French King Henry II was wounded in the eye and neck by his opponent's lance -it penetrated his golden jousting helmet, hence '*armour of gold*', the lions are the decorations on the men's shields. He died a cruel death from the two wounds 'eye and neck' as foretold in the quatrain.

MIN: Excellent analysis Dee, take three merit points.

DEE: Thank you.

MEIL: (*bored*) I just don't get why we spend so much time on the quatrains?

MIN: Meil, your rudeness today is particularly irritating; would someone care to enlighten her as to why we study the quatrains?

WIZ: (*instantly and enthusiastically*) The quatrains are pivotal to our existence, each quatrain....

MIN: (*silencing her*) Someone other than Wiz?

ROCK: The quatrains provide guidance to our existence, they foretold the end of the old world and the development of the New World Order.

FOX: So...?

LUCE: So, the comprehensive study of such is key to our understanding of the past and preparation for the future, to ensure that we do not repeat the mistakes of the relics.

MIN: Excellent Rock and Luce, two merit points each! And Meil?

MEIL: Yes Min?

MIN: I am deducting three merit points from your progress capsule for your insubordination, and as punishment I expect a handwritten analysis of your favourite quatrain tomorrow morning.

MEIL: Handwritten? But no one has used handwriting since... well since years before the Relics perished.

MIN: Well then, it'll give you a little insight into what your ancestors spent their time doing won't it?

MEIL: Yes Min, sorry Min.

FOX: Ok that is all for this morning, Chosen dismissed.

CHOSEN: (*in unison and military fashion*) We thank our Wise for bringing the light of knowledge in to our lives and pledge to serve the New World Order without question.

The Wise exit.

ROCK: Remember everyone 10.15 in the airlock.

The space transforms into the secure airlock area of the bunker.

Act 1　　　　　SCRATCHING THE SURFACE　　　　　19

> *The Chosen enter cautiously.*
>
> *The airlock*

ROCK: Al – close the airlock.

AL: Airlock secure, Rock.

ROCK: Ok everyone we're good to go, the Wise can't hear us now.

CHOSEN: Yes Rock.

ROCK: Jam, Lion -distribute the devices.

MEIL: The communicators?

ROCK: Affirmative, Nokia, Apple, Blackberry, Samsung.

JAM: Mobile telephonics, cool.

DEE: What?

WIZ: Mobile telephones – mobile communication devices available on a variety of networks enabling relics to talk to each other, send messages and other data.

CUB: Relics?

MEIL: Those that came before. Do you ever pay attention in lessons Cub?

> *Jam distributes the communicators*

ROCK: Activate the light.

> *the lights on the mobile devices slowly come into view*

ROCK: Got it?

CHOSEN: GOT IT!

ROCK: Hold it high for a signal.

> *they hold the devices above their head*

MEIL: I got a signal – I bar.

HAM: 2 bars!! 2 bars!

JAM: 2 bars and rising…..

ROCK: We must be close……anyone else?

DEE: GPRS???

POP: Me too…..well weird!

LIS: 3 bars and counting….

BEC: Me too!

ROCK: Everyone set?

CHOSEN: Yes set.

ROCK: And SYNC!!!!

MEIL: Navigate to…… wazzat?

ROCK: Navigate? You got navigate?

MEIL: Yeah says here Navigate…

ROCK: Press it!

MEIL: Are you sure that this is what the Relics did?

ROCK: Course I am, do you doubt me?

MEIL: No Rock, course not…..(*pressing button*) Place of interest, Food, Leisure, Education?

ROCK: Education.

MEIL: What do I put?

HAM: What did they call the places of Education?

JAM: Prisons! *(laughs).*

ZEE: Schools, colleges, Universities ….

KEL: Spends too much time with The Wise does Zee!

ZEE: I just like to know things that's all.

LOIS: Leave her alone Kel.

MEIL: Rock?

ROCK: Select closest.

MEIL: Ok here goes…… and sync.

DEE: I got it.

POP: Cool, me too.

ROCK: ok guys this is it…..prepare to journey!

KEL: 13 minutes to destination.

ZEE: This is mental.

LION: Gonna be great….

HAM: Gotta stay together everyone, right?

CHOSEN: Right.

HAM: The lands are gonna look different, so we need to trust the navigate.

LIS: She's right, we need to follow the directions, but the landmarks will be different than learnt.

JAM: Changed….

DEE: Yeah course they will have derr!!!!

HAM: The old maps are useless!

LIS: Not useless - just a guide. They will point us in the right direction, but the land will look different.

JAM: But is it safe?

LUCE: Safe? Course it's safe The Wise scratch the surface all the time.

JAM: I mean do we need protection?

ILY: The Wise have declared the surface free from rays, therefore it must be safe.

DEE: That may be, but no Chosen have been allowed to visit yet.

ROCK: They just want to keep it for themselves that's all, but how can we learn if we don't go to the surface?

WIZ: Well, I've got loads of questions for one!

DEE: So, have I, the Wise keep, things from us - I'm sure of it.

KEL: We must remember the Wise still value the old world and are over protective about the memories.

MEIL: You haven't told anyone what we're planning have you Kel? Cos if you have I swear I'll do for you!

ROCK: Cut it out Meil NO VIOLENCE! You know what the Wise say…. That's what ended the old world.

MEIL: Well I for one think the old world was probs a bit boring anyways…. So there!

KEL: I haven't said anything, so there you go Meil - Satisfied?

POP: Are we going to get on with this or what? We'll be out of signal soon and there will be no point.

LIS: She's right, and we don't want the Wise to wake and find us missing do we?

POP: Certainly not, else it will have all been a waste of time.

JAM: Are you sure you know the portal code Rock?

ROCK: Yes, told you I did. Zee said one of the Wise let it slip, it's a numerical format of the end date.

POP: End date?

ZEE: You know the day the surface became infected.

HAM: Diseased.

DEE: Evacuated.

LION: Dead.

CUB: Don't you're scaring me.

WIZ: End date – Battle of civilization, end of the old world – leading to mass infection of earth and relocation of The Wise and Chosen below ground in preparation for the New World Order.

ILY: Get you Wiz!

WIZ: I just like to know things, its important.

LIS: Like she swallowed one of those things the Wise go on about!

HAM: A dictionary.

Act 1   SCRATCHING THE SURFACE

WIZ: (*getting carried away*) Dictionary, a book, website or resource providing definitions of words...

sighs and groans

Luce: (*butting in*) Can we just get on with it?

Rock: Approach the portal, Jam you take the rear and keep check. Zee stay close we need to activate the code. Now everyone, quickly and quietly so as not to disturb the Wise.

ZEE: Yes Rock.

ROCK: Zee – punch in the code.

ZEE: 22-07-2022

BEC: Listen for the release....

AL: I can hear the air rush.

JAM: Stand back everyone.

ROCK: Jam, turn the cog.

JAM: It's really tough, Zee help me push it.

There is a loud creaking noise followed by an alarm sounding.

MEIL: Rock what's happening?

ROCK: There must be a backup alarm.

LIS: What are we going to do?

ROCK: The Wise will have been alerted! Jam collect the devices quickly and hide them.

MEIL: We're going to be for it now, the Wise will be angered!

CUB: I'm scared Meil.

ROCK: Don't worry Cub just follow my lead....

JAM: I won't let them hurt you Cub, I'm not scared of them.

The Wise enter

MIN: What's going on? (*seeing ROCK*) Ah, I see we've been doing a little investigating have we - Rock? (*to FOX*) Fox de-activate the alarm.

FOX: Alarm deactivated.

MIN: I hope that you have a good reason for being here? You are all very aware that entering the airlock is forbidden territory.

ROCK: (*Obviously not telling the truth*) We were just err .. playing hide and seek Min and were err.... trying to find new places to hide.

FOX: Rock, you know that this area is restricted, and any breach of rules is a serious offence.

MIN: How did you know the access code?

ZEE: We just sort of guessed.

MIN: Don't lie to me – who told you the code?

MEIL: What's it matter how we know, we have every right to go there we live here too.

WIZ: Careful Meil, don't upset them.

FOX: The access code is for your own protection Meil. We have made great sacrifices to keep you safe, many would have liked to be in your position.

MEIL: So you always say, but what are we being protected from you never explain it?

FOX: You are the Chosen – the future leaders of the New World Order.

MEIL: There you go again same old story, when will you tell us the truth?

MIN: I don't know what you mean, truth?

DEE: The truth about the old world and why we are the Chosen ones?

MIN: You know the truth; this is explained in lessons! The old world was not safe after the Final War, it was destroyed, you the Chosen were taken underground to protect you from infection, to be relocated once the new world was safe for occupancy.

DEE: So you keep saying, but you never tell us why we are the Chosen, or when we will be able to go to the surface? We need to know Min, it's not fair!

MIN: So, you were going to attempt to scratch the surface yourselves, were you?

KEL: Fantastic! Way to go Dee, we might as well give up now.

Silence

MIN: I asked a question – were you intending to scratch the surface?

Silence

MIN: Cat got your tongue now Dee? You might as well tell me the truth now.

DEE: Yes Min, sorry.

MIN: Yes Min, Sorry…What?.

DEE: Yes, we were trying to scratch the surface Min.

AL: Sorry Min,

CHOSEN: Sorry, yes, sorry.

FOX: Sorry… SORRY? Do you realise how dangerous that could be without protection? Your actions could have infected all of us!

MIN: Rock - I suspect this was your idea? Always rushing in without considering the consequences!

LIS: What consequences, we know that *YOU* have already scratched the surface.

JAM: We know you've done it more than once, we heard you talking.

MIN: You did, did you?

FOX: We have to assess the risks before giving access to the Chosen, we can't risk an outbreak, or the New World would be threatened.

MIN: Don't you see what you've done? Your stupidity could have placed our entire future at risk.

MEIL: Well maybe if you were more honest with us then we wouldn't be so curious.

MIN: And maybe if you were more respectful, no one would be placed in danger!

General discussion

FOX: Quiet! This is getting us nowhere. (*quietly to MIN*) At least they didn't scratch the surface, so nothing is compromised. Now if they promise not to do it again maybe we can all get some rest.

ROCK: But we want to scratch the surface, there are so many questions.

ILY: Like what's a flower?

LUCE: What does rain feel like?

BEC: And in London are all the streets really paved with gold?

CUB: What?

BEC: The streets in London, they're paved with gold.

JAM: That's a fairy tale you numpty!

BEC: How do you know, have you been there?

JAM: Well no of course not but I'm pretty sure.

MEIL: I think it's time you shared it with us Min.

ROCK: We just wanted to find out for ourselves what it's like on the surface.

MIN: Of all the Selfish, ungrateful, naïve …

FOX: (*interrupting*) Min, this is clearly not going to deter them, perhaps it's time we told them?

MIN: (*attempting to silence her*) They're not ready Fox. It's too soon, we still need to secure the way forward.

FOX: There is never a right time Min. If we are honest they may

Act 1   SCRATCHING THE SURFACE   27

> understand our reasons, then they may choose not to scratch the surface until the time is right.

MIN: I'm not sure Fox it's a lot to take in, what if they still decide to go up there? Everything will be ruined, a lifetime of work and nothing to show for it.

FOX: I think that's a chance we'll have to take Min.

MEIL: Well this sounds interesting, I'd like to hear it, whatever it is!

ILY: Me too

HAM: Definitely

BEC: Bout time

POP: And me

AL: Count me in

> *They all start to chatter*

MIN: Silence! As you wish, go prepare yourselves and we will meet in the assembly area in one hour.

> *Continued general excitement.*

FOX: Calm down and show some respect.

MIN: Unless I am completely satisfied that you have the maturity to process the information I will not proceed.

MEIL: Yes, Min – sorry. We're ready I promise.

MIN: I sincerely hope so Meil otherwise the repercussions could be costly to us all.

> *the Chosen exit*

FOX: I know you have concerns Min, but they are determined to seek the truth, its better coming from us.

MIN: I'm not convinced Fox; the disclosure could threaten the future of the New World Order and all that we have worked for could be in jeopardy.

FOX: We need to trust the quatrains and have faith in our teaching, we have provided them with the tools it is now time for them to make their own decisions. Come Min, we must prepare the way.

MIN: And if they rebel?

FOX: Rebellion is not an option!

The WISE exit

The space reverts back to the Assembly Room.

MIN and FOX are waiting in the Assembly Room. ROCK knocks (offstage).

MIN: Enter

ROCK enters

ROCK: The hour is upon us and the Chosen ones seek permission to enter the assembly area.

FOX: Permission Granted.

ROCK: We thank you.

FOX: And Rock, usual assembly protocol or else the meeting will be aborted.

ROCK: Yes Fox, understood. *(she signals to the CHOSEN to enter which they do in uniform fashion).*

MIN: Welcome Chosen, state your pledge.

CHOSEN: We thank our Wise for bringing the light of knowledge in to our lives and pledge to serve the New World Order without question.

FOX: At ease. *(they relax).* It is interesting that you have all pledged to serve the New World Order without question, however it is your questioning that has led to this meeting is it not?

KEL: We are only questioning because....

MIN: Silence! The meeting will take the form of a lesson and the

Chosen will only speak when addressed directly, understood?

CHOSEN: Understood.

The 'lesson' is again faced paced as the CHOSEN enact each quatrain with military precision.

FOX: Let's begin. Quatrain 51?

LIS: The blood of the just will be demanded of London
Burnt by fire in the year '66
The ancient Lady will fall from her high place
And many of the same sect will be killed.

MIN: Context?

POP: The quatrain predicts The Great Fire of London in 1666. The ancient lady refers to the fall of St. Paul's Cathedral. The fire destroyed 75 percent of the City of London.

FOX: Quatrain 24?

ZEE: Wild men, ferocious with anger, crossover rivers. The greater part of the battlefield will be against Hister;
In armour of steel the great army will make the assault,
When the child of Germany shall heed no one.

MIN: Context?

DEE: Nostradamus predicts the rise of Adolf Hitler and the German invasion of World War II. He uses wordplay to combine the words Hitler and Ister – the Latin name for the Danube. He informs us that the 'child' of Germany listens to no one which ultimately will be his downfall!

MIN: Quatrain 6?

BEC: Near the harbours and within two cities,
There will be two catastrophes & the like of which never seen;
Intense in torment, by a bomb incalculable human lives are ended,
Crying for help from the great God immortal.

FOX: Context?

KEL: Towards the end of the Second War an atomic bomb was dropped on the Japanese City of Hiroshima by a B-29 named the Enola Gay, this was followed by a second bomb on Nagasaki. A great mushroom cloud was formed and there was incalculable devastation and loss of life.

JAM: I thought that was OMD?

CUB: OMD?

WIZ: OMD- otherwise known as Orchestral Manoeuvres in the Dark, an 80's pop sensation known for their critical analogy of the Hiroshima bombing through their anti-war song 'Enola Gay'.

JAM: (*Sings*) Enola gay, you should have stayed at home yesterday
Oho it can't describe the feeling and the way you lied
These games you play, they're going to end it all in tears someday

laughs from members of CHOSEN

BEC: You're such an idiot Jam!

FOX: Order! Silence or you will be dismissed.

MIN: What do the three quatrains have in common?

DEE: They all foretold disasters in the old world which contributed towards the ultimate downfall of the relics.

FOX: Excellent again Dee, you really do take your studies seriously.

MEIL: I don't see what all this has to do with us not being allowed to scratch the surface?

MIN: Meil, I warned you to follow the protocol, pay attention and be silent or you will be taken to the thinking room.

MEIL: Sorry Min, I'm just curious. Please continue.

MIN: Wise throughout the world have followed the quatrains for many years, as more predictions came true greater faith was placed in the prophecies of Nostradamus, it soon became clear that we must prepare for the final war.

HAM: So there's other Wise, not just you?

FOX: Silence.

MIN: You must listen Ham, the answers will be given.

FOX: There have always been 'Wise' or else the future would have ceased to exist years ago.

MIN: The term 'Wise' has been applied to many great people over the centuries, people who have done measurable things in order to secure the future of civilisation, Astrologers, Physicists, Pharmacists, Politicians, Medics, Leaders, Healers, Thinkers, Explorers, Peacemakers, Predictors. So, in response to your question Ham, yes there are many other Wise. (*to the CHOSEN*) Examples anyone?

ZEE: Isaac Newton, Louis Pasteur, Florence Nightingale, Winston Churchill, Elizabeth Fry, Lord Nelson, Alan Turing, Edith Cavell – the list is endless.

MIN: Over the years the Wise have prepared for the Final War by 'harvesting', in order to ensure that the New World Order is successful and does not repeat the mistakes of the past.

JAM: 'Harvesting'? Surely everything will be a bit out of date by now!

ROCK: She is not referring to food Jam – just listen!

JAM: Oh yeah and what do *you* know about it?

ROCK: Err nothing, really.

MEIL: Nothing really, well that *definitely* means something then!

FOX: Silence!

MEIL: She knows something; I think it's only fair we do too?

ROCK: If you'll just listen Meil, the Wise will explain.

MEIL: Yeah but you already know, don't you? I thought you were a bit quiet when we first mentioned scratching the surface, it appears that we really do have a mole in the bunker after all.

general unrest

MIN: All right, all right calm down and let us finish or nothing will be explained!

FOX: Since the publication of the Quatrains in 1558, Wise have worked in unison to Harvest cells from other Wise in order to create the New World Order.

POP: That all sounds a bit grim, Harvest cells? What like in a test tube?

MIN: Exactly, Wise over the years have harvested cells from the greatest, most intelligent and powerful people on earth in preparation for the New World Order; and as Wise have departed the earth, their wisdom has remained in the form of cells.

JAM: And what precisely has happened to these 'cells'?

ROCK: You don't get it do you Jam?

JAM: You'll get something in a minute you sneaky little mole, pretending to be one of us and all the time reporting back to the Wise like some little spy.

MIN: Silence Jam, don't you understand it was vital that we impart our knowledge upon one of the Chosen as the Wise cannot live forever!

MEIL: And *we* can?

FOX: Well not forever but long enough to start the New World order.

ROCK: Don't you get it? We are the Chosen, we are the cells harvested from the Wise – we are the future!

BEC: This is rubbish on an epic scale! Do you really expect us to believe that we have been 'grown' in some sort of laboratory?

ROCK: Ever wondered why the 'airlock' is out of bounds? The Wise weren't scratching the surface at all - they were tending to the Chosen yet to be born, feeding them, nurturing them until the time is right. It's like when Cub joined us and before that Lion, didn't you consider how they arrived in the bunker?

MEIL: So, you're telling me that the Wise haven't scratched the surface yet.

MIN: That's not strictly true Meil, we are still harvesting.

DEE: How can you still be harvesting amongst the rays? It's not safe and the relics are all dead!

FOX: That's not strictly true either.

LIS: I'm confused.

FOX: Rock – date?

ROCK: 20th March 2017

KEL: It's 2025 – even I know that!

ROCK: It's 2017! *(She shows them her watch).*

ZEE: Hang on - If its 2017 then the end date hasn't happened yet.

WIZ: End date – Battle of civilization, end of the old world – leading to mass infection of earth and relocation of The Wise and Chosen below ground in preparation for the New World Order.

LUCE: So, if it hasn't happened yet that means that the surface is safe?

FOX: Not safe….

ILY: Does that mean we can visit?

FOX: NOT SAFE!

HAM: We can explore…..

LUCE: Yeah see all the things that we've learnt about

LION: Go to a park

AL: Go swimming

KEL: Learn to fly

AL: Watch a rock show

WIZ: *(eagerly)* Go to a library!

ROCK: Aren't you listening, it's not safe!

JAM: You would say that Moley!

ROCK: Just listen to them!

MIN: The final war has already started; we are informed that pockets of unrest are apparent all over the world, any chosen visiting the surface would jeopardise everything that we have worked for.

JAM: We'd be careful; you could go with us.

FOX: Don't you understand we are informed that the third anarchist is shortly to be in place and that signifies the end of the world, we simply can't afford to risk the future of the New World Order.

DEE: (*the significance dawning on her*) The definitive quatrain.... The third anarchist!

LION: What?

DEE: The quatrains tell of the third anarchist – the anti-christ; don't you remember?

> The Third Antichrist, the third to come, gets annihilated, war shall last for twenty-seven years,
> The heretics are all dead; all of the prisoners are now exiled,
> His body has reddened the waters, and the earth has been scorched.

POP: (*dimly*) Never mind the third who were the other two?

ZEE: Napoleon and Hitler, obviously!

LUCE: But who is the third anarchist?

ROCK: The great shameless, audacious bawler.
He will be elected governor of the army:
The boldness of his contention.
The bridge broken, the city faint from fear.

FOX: Our intelligence states that he has already been elected, therefore we are now operating at the highest levels of security in order to protect the New World. It is not safe for you to scratch the surface now, such actions could destroy centuries of work and preparation; and ultimately prevent the future in its entirety!

MIN: So now you know, you are the Chosen , not only chosen but nurtured to be our future leaders! Your role is vital; you have the highest honor bestowed upon you. Please do not jeopardise the future with you own selfish wish to visit what will soon be passed.

FOX: We can say no more, the rest is up to you.

Curtain

www.ingramcontent.com/pod-product-compliance
Lightning Source LLC
Chambersburg PA
CBHW050048080526
44586CB00014B/1504